QEB Write On

Katie's Mom is a Mermaid

Copyright © QEB Publishing, Inc. 2005

Published in the United States by
QEB Publishing, Inc.
23062 La Cadena Drive
Laguna Hills, CA 92653
www.qeb-publishing.com

Library of Congress Control Number 2005921263

ISBN 1-59566-101-8

Written by Hannah Ray
Designed by Alix Wood
Illustrated by Dawn Vince

Series Consultant Anne Faundez
Publisher Steve Evans
Creative Director Louise Morley
Editorial Manager Jean Coppendale

Printed and bound in China

 Write On

Katie's Mom is a Mermaid

Hannah Ray

QEB Publishing, Inc.

There's a new girl in my class,
Her name is Katie Lou,
Her hair is shiny, all golden curls,
Her eyes are sparkly blue.

Best friends with new girl Katie,
Is what I'd like to be,
But her life sounds so fantastic,
Would she be friends with me?

5

She says her mom's a mermaid,
Who sings in an ocean band.
An octopus plays the drums,
You can hear him on dry land.

Her dad's a famous cowboy,
Who rides a big white horse.
He gallops through the wild, wild west,
Catching outlaws, of course!

Katie's granny is a pilot,
Wearing goggles and a scarf.
She loops the loop and wiggles her wings,
To make the people laugh.

Her brother is a strongman,
Although he's only three,
Lifting elephants on one hand,
For all the world to see.

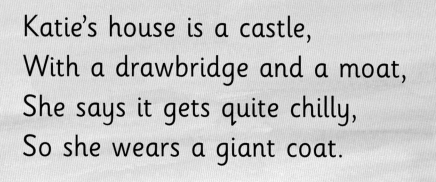

Katie's house is a castle,
With a drawbridge and a moat,
She says it gets quite chilly,
So she wears a giant coat.

There are butlers and a gardener,
A driver and a cook,
So grand it is, that Katie says,
A queen came to take a look.

10

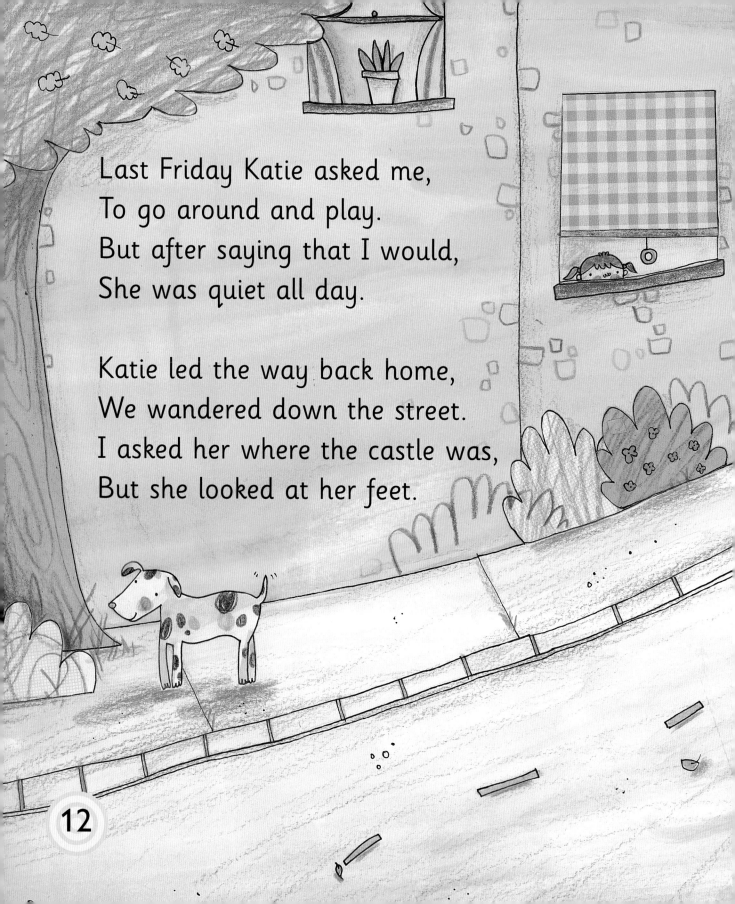

Last Friday Katie asked me,
To go around and play.
But after saying that I would,
She was quiet all day.

Katie led the way back home,
We wandered down the street.
I asked her where the castle was,
But she looked at her feet.

And when we got to Katie's house,
What a big shock I had!
A house like mine, with a bright red door,
Opened by Katie's dad.

A regular guy, not a cowboy,
Her dad delivers mail.
And Katie's mom, I soon found out,
Has legs and not a tail.

15

Katie's brother played with toys,
He showed me his best bear.
And her granny was just like mine,
Though she did have bright pink hair!

But Katie still looked worried,
"I'm very sorry," she said.
She looked like she might start to cry,
Her face was very red.

17

Katie said, in a tiny voice,
"I told a fib or two,
But I wanted you to like me,
It's hard being brand new!"

But I am just like Katie,
I love to play pretend,
And now we are two princesses,
And are the best of friends!

19

What do you think?

What words would you use to describe Katie?

Can you remember what Katie says about her mom?

Which member of Katie's family does she say is a pilot?

How does Katie describe her house?

21

Was Katie's house
really a castle?
What did it look like?

Why do you
think Katie is
quiet when her
friend has
agreed to come
and play?

Katie's dad wasn't really a cowboy. Can you remember what job he did?

Why did Katie make up stories about her family and her home?

23

Parents' and teachers' notes

- Look at the cover of the book and talk about the illustration. Read the title of the book. What does your child think the book will be about?

- Read through the book together, but stop when you reach the end of page 13. Can your child guess what happens next? Talk about the different things that could happen, and then read to the end of the story.

- Look through the book and find words that rhyme, e.g., "band" and "land." Help your child think of other words that rhyme, for example, "sand" and "hand." After you have explored these words verbally, write all the rhyming words from the story on individual cards. Place the cards face up on the table and help your child match up the rhyming pairs.

- Which is your child's favorite character in the book? Why?

- Talk about the thought bubbles in the illustrations. Why are some of the pictures in thought bubbles?

- How would your child feel if he or she were Katie's friend? Would he or she be upset that Katie made up stories?

- Encourage your child to talk about the members of his or her family. What do they look like? What jobs do they do? Does your child have any brothers or sisters? What do they like to do?

- Encourage your child to use his or her imagination to think of other things that members of his or her family could do or be. Maybe a younger brother might be an astronaut? Or a grandparent could be a lion tamer?

- Remind your child what he or she thought the book was going to be about, just from looking at the cover. How was the book different from your child's expectations?

- Ask your child if he or she likes to dress up and pretend. What games does he or she like to play?

- What is the name of your child's best friend? Can your child draw a picture of himself/herself with his or her best friend?

24